OTHER PEOPLE'S LIVES

By the same author

Poetry
The Habit of Flesh
Finglas Lilies
No Waiting America
Internal Exiles
Leinster Street Ghosts
Taking My Letters back
The Chosen Moment
External Affairs
The Venice Suite
*That Which is Suddenly
    Precious*

Novels
Night Shift
The Woman's Daughter
The Journey Home
Emily's Shoes
A Second Life
Father's Music
Temptation
The Valparaiso Voyage
The Family on Paradise Pier
The Fall of Ireland
Tanglewood
The Lonely Sea and Sky
An Ark of Light

Young Adult Novel
New Town Soul

Short Stories
Secrets Never Told

Collaborative Novels
Finbar's Hotel
Ladies Night at Finbar's Hotel

Plays
The Lament for Arthur Cleary
Blinded by the Light
In High Germany
The Holy Ground
One Last White Horse
April Bright
The Passion of Jerome
Consenting Adults
The Ballymun Trilogy
    1: From These Green Heights
    2: The Townlands of Brazil
    *3: The Consequences of
        Lightning*
Walking the Road
The Parting Glass
Tea Chests & Dreams
*Ulysses (a stage adaptation of
    the novel by James Joyce)*
Bang Bang
Last Orders at the Dockside
The Messenger

Author photograph © Brian Meade

Born in Dublin in 1959, the novelist, playwright and poet Dermot Bolger is one of Ireland's best-known writers. His fourteen novels include *The Journey Home*, *A Second Life*, *Tanglewood*, *The Lonely Sea and Sky* and *An Ark of Light*. In 2020 he published his first collection of short stories, *Secrets Never Told*. His debut play, *The Lament for Arthur Cleary*, received the Samuel Beckett Award. His numerous other plays include *The Ballymun Trilogy*, charting forty years of life in a Dublin working-class suburb; and most recently, *Last Orders at the Dockside* and an adaptation of James Joyce's *Ulysses*, both staged by the Abbey Theatre. His ninth poetry collection, *The Venice Suite: A Voyage Through Loss*, appeared in 2012. He devised the best-selling collaborative novels *Finbar's Hotel* and *Ladies Night at Finbar's Hotel*, and edited numerous anthologies, including *The Picador Book of Contemporary Irish Fiction*. A former Writer Fellow at Trinity College Dublin, Bolger writes for Ireland's leading newspapers, and in 2012 was named Commentator of the Year at the NNI Journalism Awards. In 2021 he received The Lawrence O'Shaughnessy Award for Poetry.

dermotbolger.com

OTHER PEOPLE'S LIVES

Dermot Bolger

NEW ISLAND

OTHER PEOPLE'S LIVES
First published in 2022 by
New Island Books
Glenshesk House
10 Richview Office Park
Clonskeagh
Dublin D14 V8C4
Republic of Ireland
www.newisland.ie

Print ISBN: 978-1-84840-843-2
eBook ISBN: 978-1-84840-844-9

British Library Cataloguing in Publication Data. A CIP catalogue record for this book is available from the British Library.

Typeset by JVR Creative India
Cover design by New Island Books
Printed by SPRINT-print, sprintprint.ie
Photographs in this book are © Dermot Bolger
Cover image © Peter O'Doherty

New Island received financial assistance from The Arts Council (An Chomhairle Ealaíonn). Dublin, Ireland.

New Island Books is a member of Publishing Ireland.

10 9 8 7 6 5 4 3 2 1

For Diarmuid and Donnacha, and for Helen.

Contents

Other People's Lives

I
Begin Again

The Unguarded Moment

At my age, the hardest part of restarting to write poems
Are the terms and conditions in the zero-hours contract.

Prose may be ground out on dreary Tuesday afternoons,
But you must let poems ambush you when least expected,

On a street corner or midway down a supermarket aisle,
In the unguarded moment when you find yourself writing

Without being aware that you are even trying to write;
When a single thought sparks with a jolt of electricity

That short circuits all cognisance of any task you are at
And ignites the dry undergrowth in your subconscious,

Undergrowth that lay dormant during years of drought,
Waiting for a wind to blow up, for a random stranger,

Lost in thought on a parched headland of yellow gorse,
To carelessly toss aside a smouldering cigarette butt.

Heron and Poet

Beneath the bridge, both statuesque,
It's just you and I, one mid-stream, one
Anonymous on this briar-strewn path.

Both seemingly inert, but equally alert
For any fleeting image, any darting trout
That might try to flit past our patient eye.

II
One Life

Valley Hotel,
Woodenbridge,
Co. Wicklow:

29 . 8 . 44

Mr. H Bolger,

To bread *illegible*   4 - 1 = 0

"   "   4 - 1 = 0

8 - 2 - 8

2

apples

8   4 .

The Valley Hotel, Woodenbridge, 1944

August sunlight dapples the orchard behind the hotel,
Its proprietor so besotted by my mother's bliss
That he insists on picking a bag of apples as a gift
For her to enjoy with her groom on the journey back,
From the luxury of this brief honeymoon, to embark
On the mysteries of married life in a small attic flat,
In the house in Herbert Place where Elizabeth Bowen
Spent childhood winters gazing down at a canal lock.

My mother accepts his parting gift with a shy smile,
Then the hotelier's wife appears, piqued by jealousy
At such attention bestowed on a bride who, by day,
Worked in the Moira Hotel as a mere chambermaid.
She grabs the bill from her husband with sour spite,
Altering it before it is shoved into my father's hands.

Few reminders survive from a marriage foreshortened
By her brain tumour. But all his life my father kept
This bill, cherishing the secret encrypted in a receipt,
Written by an hotelier, then changed by his enraged wife;
The jealous stabs of her pen adding, as an addendum,
Two extra shillings for this unsolicited gift of apples,
A surcharge for my mother's captivating ebullience.

How young they are back then, how little they know of life
Despite his ship being attacked on treacherous voyages,
Despite her guarding secrets only shared with her sisters.
In this moment their future is a blank canvas of joyfulness
As they depart the hotel, bags packed, to walk to the station.

Let us leave them there, luxuriating in that sunlit air,
Lips tasting of kisses, foreheads bent so close they touch
As they study the bill, then gaze at each other and laugh.

The Broken Bread Van

Allow me to introduce myself, Grandfather.
Fate never permitted us to get acquainted,
Though surely my imminent arrival was noted
By the mourners who attended your funeral,
Just weeks before a midwife delivered me.

Was I referred to as a sign of consolation
As all your emigrant offspring returned
To mix at the graveside with neighbours
Who drew comfort, amid the burial rites,
From the fresh start offered by my birth,
Wondering if I might inherit your features
And what journeys life would take me on.

Your children mostly took the same journey:
A rickety bus from Castleblaney to Dundalk,
Then the train to rented flats in a Dublin
That offered ill-paid jobs but enough freedom
To fall in love. They knew their only possibility
Of raising families was to emigrate and clock in
For long shifts in Leicester or Luton factories,
Where hands once skilled at winnowing chaff
Grew accustomed to assembling Vauxhall cars.

You turned fifty before you inherited the farm
And could marry, making up for lost time
In a fraught contest against your ageing body
To father eleven children who knew you only
As an old man. Your sole excursions to Dublin

Were to attend wedding breakfasts in the café
Opposite the church beside Westland Row Station.
You crossed that wide street with them twice:
Once in the morning, descending church steps
Amid confetti, congratulations and photographs,
And later, at dusk, when all the wedding party
Left the café to accompany the bride and groom
To the station to catch the boat train to England.

Your train home charted your known universe,
Ticking off a smudge of lights at each small town:
Skerries and Balbriggan, Drogheda and Dundalk.
Then Hackballscross, Cullaville, Annadrummond:
Villages that drew your bus closer to Castleblaney –
A town sufficiently big to conduct any business in.
Three more miles to Annyalla, the lane to the farm
Seeming ever steeper, but rising through fields
You'd tilled for decades to one day call your own.
After each child's wedding you felt more exhausted,
Glad to be back, inspecting the byre and haggard,
The shed door only you knew the knack of locking,
The darkness broken by lamplight from the kitchen.
Here was the sanctuary of home, but did part of you
Yearn to see wider worlds that existed out there,
Further even than the cities your children lived in?
Worlds so vast as to be beyond your comprehension,
But which unknown grandchildren might explore:
The grandchildren whom you knew were too young
To truly remember you, amidst vague recollections
Of having endured treks to a hillside farm to meet
A smiling old man who only travelled in his mind.

Your features did not disappear from this earth
The day I was at your funeral while in the womb.

Scattered descendants mimic your mannerisms
In London tower blocks and Bedfordshire estates.
At dusk a young woman who possesses your eyes
Stares from the balcony of a Southmere high-rise
In Thamesmead, London, surveying evening traffic:
Her gaze mirroring an unknown great grandfather.

Not everyone left. Descendants still work those fields;
The kin with whom you would have most in common
If you returned to walk your acres, shrewdly observing
Advancements in irrigation and increased milk yields.
But maybe you and I also possess some shared traits,
Both voyagers who have travelled mainly in our minds,
Even if the imaginative journeys that I embark upon
Might not fit your definition of an honest day's labour.
But you were similarly not averse to concocting fiction,
Shaving five years off your age in the census returns
You had to fill in, because your mother, the householder,
Could not read or write, but still exercised ownership
Over those fields, making you endure a lonesome wait
To bring under that roof the bride who would bear
Those eleven children. Your delayed race to procreate
Exhausted her and transformed you into an old man,
Shuffling to the doorway to watch your youngest son
Busy himself with the daily tasks now beyond you,
Cows to be milked, fields ploughed in neat furrows.

He wisely declines your feeble offers of assistance,
Leaving you free to hobble towards a makeshift den
He has constructed to let you enjoy what time remains.
The master in the village school claims to believe
That one day men in a capsule will reach the moon.
You wonder if their contraption will look any stranger
Than this one which you summon strength to enter

After using two walking sticks to cross the yard.
With time to finally travel, in your mind at least,
You climb up into the cab of a broken bread van,
Its engine clapped out like you, its frame sawn in two,
To use the back half as a coop where hens can roost.

Only the driver's seat remains in this tiny sanctum
In which you pass each day, out of people's way,
Watching down over sloping fields and drumlins,
To see what neighbours might traverse the road
To Clontibret and wonder about their business there.
I like to imagine you peering through the windscreen
Of that amputated chassis, propped up on old blocks,
Its back jammed to a gable to keep out wind and rain,
Your shrewd gaze alert to any passing cart or cyclist,
Any morsel of gossip, but also distractedly drifting off,
During intervals when the road is bereft of all traffic.
I wonder if your mind conjured up streets in Zanzibar,
Crowded souks in Tangiers, bustling Persian bazaars,
Ships in the Dutch East Indies unloaded at dawn,
Men harvesting cinnamon in Ceylon from soil as red
As the seal on royal decrees once issued in Siam?

All the places you never saw, stored in your mind
To be explored in dotage, ensconced in a broken van.
Imaginary excursions embarked on during daily waits
For the postman's bike to slowly inch up the steep hill
With letters from England; for the conceited vet to seek
His fee in guineas; for death to commence its ascent
To the yard where you wait, walking sticks at the ready
To unhurriedly walk to confront him in your own time,
Accepting how you will never hold your unborn grandson.

Found Poems in Telegrams and Letters

```
6 II 59.1Ø.29AM. FINGLAS DUBLIN
TO MR ROGER BOLGER C/O MV DUNDALK
BERTHED LIVERPOOL PRINCES DOCK
```

It isn't easy for poetry to be conjured
When each extra word inflates the cost
And punctuation is an extravagance
On the wages he can afford to post home.

My father paces the deck of a ship docked
In a foreign port, scanning wet cobbles,
Anxious for any sight of a telegram boy
Who might deliver news that his wife
Has given birth to a daughter or son,
Cloistered with her sister and a midwife
In the back bedroom where I was born.

```
BABY BOY BOTH
SPLENDID LOVE = BRIDIE
```

A found poem, nonasyllabic, in six words.

My eldest sister is considered sufficiently grown up
To entrust with the task of being sent to proffer
My mother's concise words and the requisite coins
To the officious scrutiny of the stern postmistress.

This custodian of what had been a rural post office
Before Finglas grew overwhelmed by new estates,

Tots up each allotted letter in the communiqué,
To be priced against the coins laid on the counter
Before she will permit the telegraph wire to hum.

One hour later a Royal Mail boy is dispatched
To deliver to the dockside the printed telegram.
He cadges a tip from my father on the gangplank
Who formulates in reply his own found poem:
A seven-word decasyllable for various prying eyes
To scrutinise before it reaches his wife at home.

> 6 11 59 2.38PM LIVERPOOL G 15
> TO BOLGER, FINGLAS PARK, DUBLIN.

Their love is telegraphed in sixty-two characters,
With thirteen extra spaces allowed for no charge.
Endearments curtailed, knowing they must pass
Through numerous operators required to bridge
The space between two bodies in different beds.

> DELIGHTED WITH NEWS
> ALL MY LOVE = ROGER

I don't possess his letter to her after my birth,
Though I can envisage the blue lines to denote
The envelope being stamped as registered post,
And containing, amid crisp English banknotes,
Regrets that his hope of shore leave is dashed.

But, miraculously, her reply back has survived.
A letter liberated from all the fraught restraint
Of words being counted, emotion held in check.

Well, my own darling Rogie,
Here I am up and knocking around the house.
Already as thin after just six days as ever I was.

If her simple words are not found poetry, then what is?
Break each sentence into any enjambment you want:
Orchestrate septet or sestet structures, toy with fonts,
But no realignment can disrupt her outrush of love.

Well now, our own little man was baptised today.
Dermot Patrick Mary. The nuns sent me word.
I put Mary in his name because of the Marian Year.
He looked so lovely: a sweet lad and very little trouble.
I felt really proud of him as the nurse carried him out
To the taxi to be brought to church by his Godmother.
I stayed home until my turn comes to be churched
When the priest feels I'm ready to receive his blessing.

She hoped I'd be a priest. She might be unimpressed
To discover she gave birth to a quizzical agnostic
Who served no useful apprenticeship, learnt no trade
Except how to live on my thin sliver of imagination,
In this world she would find as unfathomably alien
As her unquestioning religiosity feels foreign to me.

I am excited to have Dermot's baptism over, even though
I also feel a bit tired and weak. This is only my sixth day.
But I'll be finished with the nurse's visits in the morning
And when you get home I'll be as strong as ever I was.

The joyous half of their story exists in these lines:
A sailor at sea always trying to make it home,
Even for just one hour before his ship sails again.

A love embedded in hurried lines, coded telegrams.
Perhaps distance helps keep their romance so fresh.
We children never truly know when he is due home,
But pick up signs, lipstick donned, a fire set ablaze
In the front parlour we are suddenly barred from.

Well, my darling, I know you'll be home when you can.
I'll be glad to see my Rogie when you are allowed come.
I love you, darling, with all my heart and hope and pray
That your two sons will be as good as their good father.

Her words lack any inkling that within ten years
The woman writing them with such tenderness
Was to die at Christmas. All that would remain
Is this letter, waiting to be found decades later;
With her own words now being typed by the son
Whom she watched being taken away by taxi
To an empty church to be solemnly baptised,
In a ceremony she herself was excluded from.
I intersperse her surviving words with mine
Six decades after they were hurriedly composed
By a mother anxious to catch the evening post;
Our sentences interlace as if they could bridge
The chasm across which our hands cannot clasp.

My sweetheart, I'll say no more now as I do feel tired.
I have your letter and feel so disappointed you may not get home.
Still where there is life there is hope so I 'll keep up my heart.
Well darling Rogie goodbye. The children are all splendid today.
They enjoyed a lovely dinner and everything of the best.
It does take money, God knows, but my darling sees to that.
Love and XXX to my own Rogie from your Bridie.

For decades I have crafted poetry, slow draft after draft,
But I will never write a love poem as pure as her letter,
Where words spill out so easily, flowing from the heart.

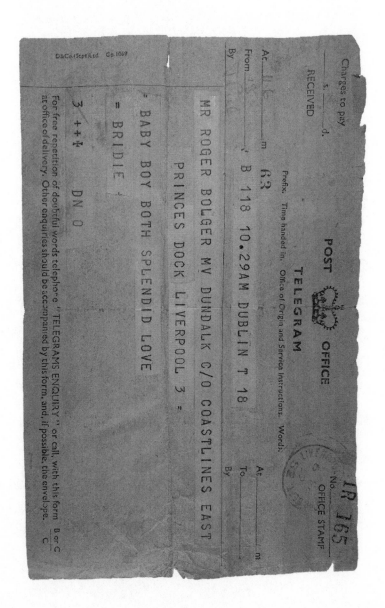

My Teacher Recites a William Allingham Poem

Four ducks on a pond,

I had thought the first poem I heard was by Ledwidge
Or Monsignor Pádraig de Brún's deft embezzlement
Of Gogarty's verses about a ship from Valparaiso.

A grass-bank beyond,

But, in a makeshift classroom in a church basement
Where light barely penetrated windows of plate-glass,
I now realise that this was the first poem I recollect
Being recited by my teacher, whose life was cut short.

A blue sky of spring,

Mr Donnelly's voice paused after reading the last line.
Aged nine, I was perplexed by its mysterious simplicity,
By why anyone would record so insignificant a moment.

White clouds on the wing;

'This is the simplest poem you'll ever read,' he said,
'Maybe one day, if old enough, you'll understand it.'

What a simple thing

As my teacher never attained the age of Christ
I have no way to convey how my life panned out;
With crescendos of bliss and bitter heartache

To remember for years –

Punctuating the journey bringing me to this age
Where, whenever I recall being a puzzled child
In a cellar lit by stray flecks of coloured sunlight,

To remember with tears!

I wish to raise my hand across the years to declare,
'I think I grasp it now. I understand the poem, Sir.'

The Night Bakery

I try but fail to remember the name of the girl I met;
Only how the taste of cigarette smoke and lipstick,
When we kissed in a lane off Grafton Street,

Amply justified my decision to miss the last bus
And walk the three miles home, instincts alert
To navigate any corners where skinheads lurked.

Dropping any hard-man pretence, I pause in my walk
At the corner where Clune Road and Jamestown meet,
Sensing this to be the place where I finally feel safe.

Part of me stands there still, decades later, sheltered
By a Griselinia hedge and by leaves of silver beech,
Staring at the Downes Butterkrust bakery gates

Where smoke wafts as bakers prepare a fresh batch.
The night air is suffused – just as I am suffused
To my soul – with airborne particles of yeast

And flour that I ingest with each exultant breath:
The aftertaste of her kiss infused with the scent
Of bread being baked on this sleeping street.

Loneliness

Even after so many years, I still can't comprehend
Why on that particular night, for no ostensive reason,
I found myself waylaid by an inexplicable loneliness.

I had a wife. Teenage sons awaited me at home.
I had a luxury suite on the Montreal waterfront
At a literary festival, about which all I can recall

Is being chauffeured to await my cue backstage.
The jaunt was meant as a respite from daily life,
From collecting my sons after swimming lessons.

So why then that night, after crossing the street
To eat in the window seat of an anonymous diner,
Populated primarily by solitary older men,

That, as the bored chef reheated my meal
And I gazed through plate-glass windows,
I became stricken by an aching loneliness?

The emotion didn't feel related to my life then;
But presaged an acute lonesomeness to come,
Which, when it arrived at an unspecified date,

Could never surpass, no matter how bad it felt,
My desolation as I sat alone in that drab eatery
Unable to rationalise my anguish or to grasp

Why it barely left me with sufficient strength
To set aside my plate, tip a disinterested waitress,
And, weary beyond exhaustion, re-cross the street,

Afraid I wouldn't reach the shelter of my hotel room,
Yet knowing that when I did, I'd remain overwhelmed
By a foretaste of some unknowable loneliness to come.

How Other People Pass Their Days

How other folk buttress their days remains a mystery.
Folk who concoct no self-imposed deadlines, no novels

Demanding to be finished, no array of opening stanzas
Arriving unexpectedly, clamouring to be written down.

It's forty-four years since I stood in a moonlit garden,
Teenage friends calling me back to a party in progress

To celebrate my debut letterpress pamphlet of poems.
But I couldn't rest, obsessed by what to write next,

By where subsequent imaginative journeys might lead.
So many novels since then, torrents of poems and plays,

But could what people mistake for versatility be perhaps
An inability to be sufficiently at ease with myself to relax,

Not as a playwright or novelist, but simply as some geezer
Able to companionably abide with the ghosts of his past,

Not irrationally convinced that if he lets down his guard
Life will fuck up, again snatching away someone he loves?

A man always acting as his own watchdog, no little boy lost
But a dervish hurtling through the vortex of his imagination

Unsure of who he might encounter in a mirror when he stops,
Torn between twin voices in his brain locked in competition:

The voice pondering which creative challenge to next take on,
And the voice asking, what phantoms are you running from?

Written in a Church in Arezzo

Nadezhda Mandelstam noted how poets, after a life tending
To intricacies of language, would, if lucky, be remembered
For one solitary lyric, a random phrase or nomadic couplet,

With all other trace of their labour being as erased by time
As the dissipated fragments of Piero della Francesca's frescoes,
The Legend of the True Cross; their panoramic sweep intact

Only in any residual memory retained in masonry cement.
I should probably sit here and marvel at his masterwork,
His ingenious use of perspective, the geometric dexterity

That bedazzled his fellow Renaissance jobbing artists
And still causes connoisseurs to catch their breath
At his extravagant vision balanced by such symmetry.

However I feel no inclination to ponder the significance
Of a hodgepodge of mythic claptrap and medieval politics
He chronicled on these walls to gratify his paymasters.

Instead my eye is drawn to the missing segments, gaps
Where the painted plaster has crumbled into chalk dust.

For me its real message is how true weight of our cross
Will only be felt when remnants of our precious memories

Bewilderingly implode, crumbling slowly like these frescoes,
Into galaxies that
                    unfathomably   diverge
        and

                                        drift
                                          a s u n der.

Never So Close

It is strange that we never seem so close
As that afternoon when you cease to know my identity;

A long dead brother perhaps, but certainly
A welcome visitor for the whiskey I manage to smuggle in.

We sit in a sunlit courtyard of a nursing home;
Two men finally with much to say to each other, because

While I spare you the distress of my news,
We now share the fate of having lost wives far too young.

As if sensing my mood, you say, 'I can't grasp
How life fell apart. Everything was grand until Bridie died.'

'That happened forty years ago, Dad,' I explain.
You look perplexed. 'Are you sure? It only feels like weeks.'

I don't reply. There is nothing to be said.
Through an open window above us, a stroke patient cries out,

Almost without hearing herself, *'Nurse! Nurse!'*
Every ten or twenty seconds, adrift in a recurrent malaise.

Her heart-rending pleas no more register
In your consciousness than if she were a blackbird or thrush.

I discreetly refill your glass with whiskey,
You conspiratorially nod your thanks. We sit there quietly,

A father and son conjoined in widowhood,
With so much in common if we could only communicate.

We share the silence of a slow July afternoon,
Peaceably, companionably, both having nowhere else to be.

Sunday Walk

For Anne

Did I ever undertake any walk equally arduous
As that Sunday, nine days after her funeral?

The afternoon heat pressed down as oppressively
As a boulder I felt eternally condemned to shoulder.

I had no conscious plan to take any particular route.
I left the house to save my sons having to witness

Their father's mute, mercilessly debilitating grief.
Yet my legs knew the pilgrim path they would trace,

Up Washerwoman's Hill and past the ancient church
To the apartment where we had known such bliss

Decades before. I knew she wouldn't be waiting there,
On the wall where we once met to view a flat for rent,

Bicycles idle beside us, our future stretching ahead.
Yet, even in her absence, I somehow grasped comfort

In recalling her excited smile back then when this wall
Became the embarkation pier for our shared adventure.

How long did I sit there, unable or unwilling to move?
Inexpressibly exhausted and bereft, though passers-by

Could not have guessed at the depth of agony I felt.
This was my lowest ebb, though on later occasions

I was similarly ambushed by grief, rendered decimated
By insignificant memories I had no defence against.

But that Sunday, after summoning strength to unsteadily
Walk home, I knew that I would survive those onslaughts.

I can't explain why this inconsequential walk was tougher
Than anything I had previously suffered or later endured.

I only know I came through it, like I know you will persevere
Through sleep-estranged nights while learning to navigate

This unmapped terrain, without compass or Northern Star.
I stake little claim to wisdom. I only know this fact because

When I got home that Sunday, I phoned the man you loved.
Who, with wise compassion, assured me I'd make it through.

I wouldn't presume to suggest you heed any words of mine;
I merely wish to pass on his steadfast reassurance to you.

Letting Go: Four Poems

1. The Dead

We see the dead as extinct particles of carbon
Or as being elevated to an enlightened status,
Released from all of the human contradictions
That governed how they navigated their lives.

We imbue them with apparent wisdom and intuition
To conjure ghostly stratagems that let them assuage
The doubts and questions still causing us anguish
By infiltrating our dreams with cryptic messages.

But if shorn of all human flaws so they only retain
The altruistic aspects of their nature, their ability
To make us feel wrapped in radiant love whenever
They were not burdened by doubt and insecurity,

Then these benevolently omniscient guardians
Cannot be the imperfect beings we cherished,
Who guarded secrets and nursed anxieties
That festered, unable to be openly addressed.

If any benign sages watch down over our lives,
They cannot be the flawed souls whose absence
We still grieve. We will have irrevocably lost them,
No matter what exalted state of grace they exist in.

2. Letting Go

To let go of the past you must begin to forgive;
Forgive those you love, but perhaps most of all

Forgive yourself, for your sake, on their behalf,
So you learn to frame every action into a prayer

Offered up not to God, but to those no longer here.

3. Ten Years On

Ten years on, unresolvable questions shouldn't still count.
I have a new life, a new love and have essentially moved on.

You appear less frequently in the backdrop of dreams.
When last you did, you fiercely gripped a steering wheel

To execute a dogged U-turn at a set of traffic lights,
Refusing to glance back, as if you sensed our attempt

To follow you and resolutely decided to shake us off.
What's over is over, in a shared life cut off in mid-flow,

And left as suspended as any unfinished sentence.
The days are rare now when I listen out for any echo

Of all that was left unsaid, answers I still need to know.

4. The Residents' Lounge

During each winter closure, the proprietor instigates
Subtle changes. He upgrades facilities, adding treats

To charm his regular guests who return like pilgrims
To luxuriate every year in the comfort assured there.

His instincts are so attuned to striking the balance
Between innovation and nostalgia, that this hotel

Only remains permanently unchanged in our minds,
And now only in my mind, a decade after your death.

If I close my eyes its layout realigns to how it once was.
We sit there, you having bagged our favoured armchairs

While I fetched complimentary post-dinner Irish coffees.
Such perfect equilibrium exists between us in this corridor

As we await our sons' thrilled footsteps, eager to display
The medals they have won in the wondrous kiddies' club.

We gaze, benignly amused, into the residents' lounge
At elderly couples sweltering in the heat of a blazing fire,

And speculate, half-jokingly, if the time will finally come
When we will wish to spend our nights seated in there,

Swapping chitchat about arthritis and hip replacements,
Surrounded by cabinets displaying rare breeds of duck

Shot on the Wexford Sloblands over fifty years before,
And preserved in there ever since, their startled stares

Trapped in formaldehyde by a long-deceased taxidermist.
Our shared life was similarly cut short in mid-flight,

So we are now preserved only in this small vignette
In which we are young and relaxed, our lives ahead,

Staring into that lounge in which we never got to sit,
In our retirement, to benignly gaze out into this corridor

At young couples who, after fussing over children all day,
Savour a moment to relax and envisage a shared old age.

Nocturne Variations

Some nights in dreams I still walk up that street
Where steeply raked terraces ascend on one side,
Opposite a counterpoint of bare factory railings,
Arrayed like blank sheet music awaiting notation.
If strangers pass me in the dark I ask for clues
As to the whereabouts of the other Dermot Bolger.
Not the teenager who struggled to find courage
To knock at a bungalow on that road and ask
If a girl he had kissed after a dance was at home.
The youth so crushed by her young sister's retort
About her being out walking with a boy named Tom
That he lost the resolve to risk further humiliation
By ever re-entering her front garden where hedgerows
Had afforded them an abundance of moonlit privacy
On the night he walked her home, her lips wondrous
Before she tore herself away, urging him to call again.

It is another Dermot Bolger that I inquire about:
The version of myself who possessed the courage
To interrogate her dismissive sister and discover
How Tom was a baby nephew she brought for walks;
My alter ego, who would have announced before I left
'Be sure to tell her I called and will keep calling back'.
Not the actual me who only discovered my mistake
Years later, meeting by chance when it was too late,
And the girl described sitting in, night after night,
Hoping I'd be brave enough to risk calling again.

I don't wish to suggest dissatisfaction with my life.
But, as I age, I grow more cognisant of other lives
I might have led if, when facing litmus test moments,
A panicked response had not made me impulsively
Strike more discordant chords than perfect octaves,
In this unfinished nocturne that pervades my sleep
Where avatars lead lives that might have been mine.

This causes occasional dreams in which I find myself
Passing those factory railings to halt at that bungalow
And wonder about the life that my assertive alter ego
Might have led if unencumbered by my shy diffidence.
What would he say, if roused from sleep by my knock
At the door of this neat house that his wife inherited,
Where they still live, eschewing emotional turbulence,
Enjoying children and careers in shrewd professions?

Perhaps he might not even see this replica of himself
Who has spent decades at desks in numerous rooms
In monasteries, lighthouses or small terraced streets,
Concocting phantoms to lead proxy lives at my behest.
He might stare past me, perplexed at my random knock,
Too preoccupied by tomorrow's routine of allotted tasks
To notice a doppelgänger with unanswerable questions.

Or would he acknowledge me, before patiently explaining
How I am merely the latest incarnation to call to his door?
Might he point to those factory railings, no longer bare,
But revealed as a latticework score of musical notation;
Each note symbolising variations of me who splintered off
Into alternate lives, but now impaled here as broken chords,
Arpeggios who believed they had broken free of the melody
Before being compelled to end on the same note as we began.

I'm too old to pretend that I can make sense of my life –
Its decisions taken or evaded, words spoken or unsaid –
But I can ask if I would be irrevocably altered at my core
If I had found the courage to court that wondrous girl
That, I imagined, had used her sister to brush me off.
Who might I have become if we'd fallen in love, or if fate
Had paired me with girls with whom I shared affairs
Before being lucky to meet the mother of my children?

Or what if caution had snared me in some spider's web
Of a pensionable job, if I'd ignored an old poet's advice
To burn every bridge and so deliberately leave myself
Qualified for nothing but casual work and blank verse?
Might I have yielded to the insidious thought process
Of gradually ceasing to see myself primarily as a poet
Stacking shelves, but as a mandarin toying with verse
Before he found serenity by swapping the ambiguity
Of poetry for a quantifiable skill like brewing craft beer?

What if I'd kept a vow to my mother to become a priest
Who eternally battled celibacy, alcohol and loneliness?
Or if I'd endured the fate I once feared might be mine,
As I felt a dread, lest I was gazing at my future self,
When I watched an old fellow factory hand clock out
To return to his bedsit where he was later found dead.

How intrinsically altered would I have been in these lives?
'As happily unhappy' as anyone, as Kavanagh remarked,
Or embittered by an inexpressible sense of unfulfillment?
Perhaps I am the sum of each self I encounter in dreams
Or do I display naivety by trying to pigeon-hole myself
As merely the leaf, blossom or bole in Yeats's great poem?

At this age my back feels like a misshapen harpsichord,
Its discordant strings coming loose from the tuning pin,
Yet my inner music continues, blessed by this benediction
Of new love. I sense movements still waiting to be composed
In this life I envisaged as a symphony, but I now perceive
To be a simple nocturne, enriched by late embellishments.

Yet my dreams still occasionally lead me to that bungalow
To stand with my double, staring in companionable silence
At that music score, only visible to us, on factory railings:
Its descending scales charting multiplicities of lives unled,
Each a variation on a theme, a modulation that diverged
As our right hand was engaged with the thematic melody,
Playing the steady crotchet beat that holds us all together,
While our left hand toyed with each abstract variation,
Adding, amid sustained minims of chords, the bass notes
And quavers which life insisted that we perform in public
While still only tentatively learning how to play the piano.

In my dreams, all these variations on myself stare back,
Pondering whether substitute versions of one another
Are wiser or happier or equally bedevilled by self-doubt;
Wondering if words, spoken aloud or only in our hearts,
Still resonate, drifting like satellite signals lost in space,
Filling the silence between notes our right hand played
As our left hand hesitated, unsure of when to come in.

Red Balloons Carried Over a Railway Bridge

I recall every detail of this exact night, thirty years ago.
Glistening ice on a tarmac lane I frantically ran down
To hail a taxi on the main road, your mother anxiously
Waiting at the door, bag packed, counting contractions.
My sense of stepping into a world about to forever change,
A new life starting, anxious hands entwined as the taxi sped
Through frosted three a.m. streets towards the hospital.
All emotions magnified – apprehension, love, expectation –
In the hours watching your mother endure labour pains,
Willingly but agonisingly; then one last push, the midwife
Lifting you aloft, telling her she had given birth to a son.

Thirty years later, here we are, a tiny convivial procession
Crossing a pedestrian bridge over a London railway track.
Your younger brother and his joyous partner hold aloft
Red birthday balloons, their strings hopelessly entangled.
No, not hopelessly: everything about today is impregnated
With hope. One presence is missing whom we would love
To be here, centre stage with you, as she was on the night
Of your birth. But other loved ones join us as we precede
Towards all that the future holds. In childhood I needed
To grip your hand, explain facts, give guidance and advice.
But this is your city now. It is you who acts as my guide
To the streets we traverse: six harmonious saunterers
Venturing to meet your friends in a new life you sculpted
For yourself with the woman whom you love. Metal rungs
Clang to the music of our feet. Laugher rises, our chatter

Inconsequential, this moment being sufficiently wondrous
That no words need saying aloud about those we miss,
Those we love and those we hope may follow behind us.

III
Other People's Lives

Nuala O'Faolain on a Bicycle on Brooklyn Bridge

'It's not just that I'm about to die,' she lamented,
'It's that every insight I gleaned will die with me.
My years of intensive reading, the years of learning
How to live my life, learning how to allow myself to
Summon courage to conquer demons of self-doubt,
To coax my voice to speak and miraculously discover
That my emotions resonated with so many others.'

Nuala, this is how I always choose to envisage you,
In a wide-brim hat such as might have been worn
By a carefree spirit, happily cycling forth to relish
Any minor curiosities she might find to cherish
In a 1950s village, dressed at its best for Fair Day.

With freshly cut flowers in your wicker basket,
You freewheel through crowds on Brooklyn Bridge
Weaving about so wildly that we need to reach out
To grasp the handlebars of a high-saddled boneshaker
And stop you careering into us, lost in blithe thought.

We mistake you for some eccentric New Yorker
Until you tilt back your oversized hat, totally at home
Over three thousand miles from home, your face
Breaking into a smile as you recognise old friends
From another world, though you made every world
Seem your own. Laughing amid the teeming crowd,
As if finding each other there is no less curious
Than casually meeting by chance on Grafton Street,
You say, 'So here we all are now, the whole lot of us.'

Fairground Ponies

In memory of the painter, Jack B Yeats

It might seem more apt to praise
Your monumental late canvases,
Where, freed from pictorial reality,
You plastered, in rich vibrant layers
The raw emotive colours of memory.
Your landscapes no longer external,
But infused, not with scenes you'd seen,
But with the tumultuous passion and grief
That such memories now conjured up,
Echoing the cathartic chaos of dreams
As they burst into such startling hues
Of jade and jasmine and kingfisher blue
That mere brushstrokes were not enough
To keep up as you moulded glistening daubs
Of paint into shape, using your fingertips.

So why do I consider your last ever sketch
To be equally wondrous? Two wooden
Fairground ponies swirl in joyous pursuit,
On a carousel designed to extract pennies
And delight from children in small towns.
Their innocent joy still engaging your mind
That remained enthralled by the breadth of life.
A frail old man propped up by heaped pillows
At the window of a Portobello nursing home:
Your fingers barely possessing the strength
To hold a pencil steady over a blank sheet,
A mere forty-eight hours before your death,
But continuing to do what came as naturally
As speech or sleep, creating faint sketches
That evoked joy, almost to your last breath.

On Hearing of the Death
of Dermot Healy

Your heart succumbs awaiting the ambulance,
          Causing this plunge into darkness.
Then, after an infinitesimal infinity,
          Your eyes unexpectedly blink open,

Unshockable, yet still receptive to wonder.
          Any sense of fear instantly suppressed:
You've woken in tighter corners than this,
          Places where palpable dangers lurked.

You never feared to confront any situation,
          A humane and fiercely-earned innocence
Being your deliberate sole weapon of choice.
          Your heart would refuse to beat faster

Even if not stopped in this unfathomable limbo.
          You remain calm, certain of nothing
Except that you recognise the voice behind you.
          Your old friend, the poet Michael Hartnett,

Whispers, *'Dermot, have you heard my latest joke?'*
          You blink again, slowly steady yourself,
In what is eternity or a last onslaught of endorphins.
          'No. But I bet you've not heard my new one yet.'

Trieste, June 2014 / Dublin, July 2020

The Novelist at Ninety-Three

At first, having to endure this endless wait made no sense,
But now, helped every afternoon into a comfortable chair

In the nursing home foyer, you realise you have become
Inadvertently trapped as a guest at some literary festival.

The pleasant but distant organisers insist on leaving you
Stranded beside your wheelchair, patiently waiting to meet

Whatever academic is scheduled to conduct the interview
After you read from your work when wheeled out on stage.

Young interns are attentive, perpetually serving you tea,
But it is the festival curators who simply don't appreciate

The wastage of writing time when you should be at your desk
Back home, painstakingly toiling on your novel-in-progress,

Whose convoluted plot seems resolutely determined to slip
Beyond your grasp, causing intense agitation and anguish;

The damned book refusing to grant you a moment's peace
Until you somehow pull together each strand to complete it.

A Tram Stop in Eastern Europe

How can I justify listing you among the women in my life?
I never knew your name. We shared no act of intimacy
Beyond a kissed cheek when my airport-bound tram came.

Yet, with many supposedly significant encounters forgotten,
I still recall becoming aware of a luminosity within you,
And your innate courtesy after you saw me, waiting alone

At a tram stop in some university town I found myself in.
Having attended my reading, you offered to wait with me,
Feeling that my departure needed some degree of ceremony.

On that quiet street you gave the only gift you could offer,
The ease of your company, while shyly sharing the hopes
You possessed as a confident twenty-year-old European.

You described your joy at holding a friend's new-born child,
Envying her sense of fulfilment, but wary of being entrapped
When you yearned to explore beyond your parents' horizons.

I've no idea where fate led you. I only recall your *joie de vivre*
As you laughed, making me conscious of keeping you late
For the bustle of your busy life. I knew that those moments

When we waited side by side, were all I would remember
From the planes and anonymous hotels of that reading tour.
You were not anonymous. Your generosity made me aware

Of unglimpsed lives in towns where I only spent one night.
I knew you would remain standing, taking time from your life,
Hand raised in salutation after my tram passed beyond sight.

A Sonnet for Isabella Lucinda Bright

On the edge of nowhere the mobile library stops
After dusk in January beside a seaside golf course.
Surely nobody awaits us on such a stormy night.

But a tiny hand appears once we open up the door,
Arthritic fingers gripping the rail sufficiently tight
To let her slowly ascend steep steps into the van.

Having accepted a lift on the back of a tractor
From her house between the links and seashore,
Radiant at ninety-one, Isabella Lucinda Bright
Bestows a weekly greeting on us library staff,

Her jest and energy banishing the wintry dark
As she asks, as usual, for two detective novels
And if we have anything by Samuel Beckett
Because his mordant wit still makes her laugh.

A Woman's Handwritten Note

Three decades after your death friends still offer me
Letters written by you as keepsakes, mementoes
Of the Eden you presided over in your final years.
But I am happy to simply possess a scribbled note
You left when I was late cycling to your bungalow,
Having paused, back when wine shops were rare,
To search for a good Chianti to bring out as a gift.
The sun was shining, other bottles already open.
Your note just read, '*Come through to the garden,*
You will find us there.' I see ancient deckchairs,
Faces turned in welcome. Your note is for me alone,
But with your garden now preserved only in my mind,
I hope you will forgive me if I have also invited
An ensemble of departed friends to meet me there.
Most will arrive before me, because as this memory
Casts me back into my twenties, I am running late
As usual, with so many tasks to attend to; my bike
So laden with books by new writers I've published
That my back wheel has buckled, slowing me down
On the steep approach to your tiny republic of love.

I know you will make my unexpected guests welcome,
Especially those recently deceased, startled to be there
Admiring your sunflowers, copper-tipped montbretia,
Your goat's beard, monkshood, tubular-shaped foxgloves,
Your chimney bellflowers and notched-petalled hollyhocks.
These dead were wandering lost until they found your note
And followed the path past your tumbledown garage
With its antiquated parked car, undriven for decades.

I have no idea how many will await me in your garden,
Some faces vivid in my mind, others half-forgotten,
Yet all are kept alive in memories I retain of them.
My logical mind is cognisant that I won't see them again
Unless perhaps in some hallucinogenic state, induced
By a lack of oxygen to my brain during my dying breath.
Yet this prospect of a millisecond reunion will suffice
As a kernel of eternity. Logic must be kept to the fore,
Yet we cannot perceive life solely through one prism
When our dreams float up from unchartable seafloors.
Perhaps actuality doesn't matter. What is of true import
Is that love still causes me to treasure a scribbled note,
A scrap of paper pinned to peeling paint on an old door.
It's immaterial if I know that nobody awaits my footsteps;
I still allow myself the luxury of imagining faces turning,
Hands raised in greeting, after I wheel my bike in the gate
To find your scrawled words, an entreaty for me to come
Straight through into the garden where I will be welcomed.

The Monday Men

Thirty years have passed since I promised myself
To bring out a camera with me early one Monday
And wait on the bench adjoining the fourth tee.
I'd coax the old men emerging through pine trees,
In companionable leisurely four-balls, to pose for me,
As they shared old jokes to stoically pass the time
While waiting for the green to clear on a par three
That they all now required rescue woods to reach
When a wedge would have sufficed in their prime.

They were the Monday men, their competition
Too informal to even print in the club calendar;
Widowers and retirees who made me welcome,
Taking time to befriend a newcomer to the club
Who was only learning the game's intricacies.
Not that the serious club golfers were unfriendly,
But their earnestness often bored me senseless,
Painstakingly lining up putts with the solemnity
Of specialists about to perform open-heart surgery.

The Monday men had survived surgery and cancer,
Many endured widowhood, loneliness or ill health;
But such topics were not alluded to amidst the banter
So I only slowly recognised the unspoken discretion
With which these elderly men looked out for each other,
Able to convey compassion, commiseration or concern
With barely any need for a single word to be exchanged.
Keepers of each other's backstories, witnesses to decline,
Competing fiercely for small side bets, while being ready

To cheer on any friend's tee-shot that found the green.
They helped each other find lost golf balls in the trees,
Stepping gingerly, with plastic hips and creaking knees.

But it was their faces that primarily fascinated me;
Faces that Fellini would have happily cast as extras,
That Pasolini would let his camera lens linger on,
That Beckett would have studied with piercing intent,
Perceiving decades of living etched in those features.
Their furrowed lines and ridges were so expressive
That it seemed, as age peeled away all vanity,
The innermost strength was brought to the surface
Of their lined faces; sculpted busts of themselves,
Monuments to endurance, survival and perseverance.

I never found the impertinence to interrupt their game
By asking those elderly golfers to pose for photographs,
But sometimes in dreams they appear on that tee-box.
Standing companionably together, while retaining
A certain distance, occupying their own separateness,
They pose with sudden shyness, anxious to crack jokes
And make light of this everyday moment, perplexed
By why anyone would wish to remember them like this.

Their photo taken, they select a club and wait in turn
To stand up on the tee, acknowledging every good shot
By an opponent in friendly rivalry, showing forbearance
At each other's foibles, at ancient jokes endlessly retold.
They linger until the last of them has driven off,
Before glancing at me in my dream to nod silently
As if no words were needed in God's waiting room.
Then, steering trollies, they descend the steep incline,
Speaking only when I'm out of earshot, but not of me,

As they repeat yarns they could finish for each other
And disappear beyond view of my subconscious,
Calmly striding towards hospices and nursing homes,
Dementia and cardiac arrest; facing without fuss
Whatever fate awaited them and may await all of us.

Sydney and Gladys

Because there is no one else left to remember
That frail, diminutive, eighty-year-old pensioner,
Her brittle bones shrunken by osteoporosis,
Who struggled every evening to help to steer
Her plump older brother up the narrow stairs
From the sitting room where he passed his days
Occupying an armchair close to the open fire,
Bowlegs barely able to take his enormous weight:
The legacy of a lifetime coping with the aftermath
Of childhood rickets: with curvature of the spine
And a forehead so enlarged it looked misshapen.

Yet his face always ready to broaden into a smile
As he proudly recalled the high point of his life:
The night when a stranger knocked at that door
And asked for him – *for him!* – by his full name.
Both his sister and he terrified in the kitchen
That somehow he had got himself in trouble
And the police suspected him of some crime;
Then his sense not just of triumph but relief,
When the stranger explained that he had won
The Evening Press 'Spot the Ball' competition.

His face beamed, perspiring with heat from the fire
As yet again he relived his elation, thirty years on,
At this besuited stranger handing him a cheque
That necessitated his first and only visit to a bank.
Always this same story, every last detail recounted.
Always the same welcome from his gracious sister,

Her face smudged with lipstick in her excitement
At having a visitor enter the self-contained world
Of that small Corporation house they were raised in.

Then her unspoken hint that it was time to leave
Because she needed to again summon the strength
To assist in his torturously slow assent up the stairs
To his childhood bedroom, the room where he was born,
Where he slept in fretful discomfiture, acutely aware
That in this house he was loved and truly belonged.

The Corporation Housing Architect
In memory, Herbert George Simms 1898-1948

In these lockdown nights of a silent pandemic,
At Halloween, when the dead supposedly walk
In remnants of shrouds and of winding sheets,
I find myself alone, opposite your former house.
Tonight not even living children have come forth
To race beneath mature trees on St Mobhi Road,
Screaming behind masks and feigning fright
At the sight of fake skeletal hands reaching up
From the lawns of these desirable 1930s properties
Bedecked in the mock paraphernalia of horror.

But even if the ghosts of every former resident
Of this street were to crowd onto the pavement,
To re-enact daily rituals from past existences,
I doubt if I would spot your unobtrusive presence
Among the throng. You were always so overlooked
That it took hours before anyone found your body
Lying on dark train tracks, alive but so mutilated
They amputated your arm when trying to save you.

You stamped an indelible imprint on Dublin city,
But are rarely remembered on this or any street.
So allow me to pause a moment outside the door
You departed from on your final morning alive,
Burdened by so much unfinished work to be done,
So many dwellings to design, yet acutely aware
That they would never be enough to house the poor
And ease Dublin's relentlessly unsolvable problems.
The weight of this responsibility besieges your mind

Along with your own ghosts. Skeletal arms reach up
From the mud of no-man's-land, trying to grab you,
Furious at the unfairness of how a train driver's son
Used his ex-serviceman's grant to study architecture,
While their mutilated corpses still lie there, unfound.

You were the sole working-class diploma student there,
Permitted to mix with social betters because you'd seen
Shell-shocked boys screaming, with amputated limbs.
You became a true rarity, an architect who understood
The reality, rather than the theory, of cramped housing,
Of shared outdoor toilets, of stampeding famished boys
Cascading down bare staircases in tenement buildings.
Nothing was theoretical for you in conferences to plan
Layout densities of estates in Cabra West or Crumlin,
Cumberland Street flats with their penny-dinner hall,
The four-storey blocks in Cook Street with hipped roofs,
Where parapets and balconies garlanded the courtyard.

Councillors always denouncing any unenumerated cost,
Cartels of sub-contractors conspiring to keep bids high,
Rings of timber merchants, coteries of cement importers.
The chief city architect never replaced after he retired
Because the Corporation had you, a useful pack mule
To ply with additional work. Seventeen thousand dwellings
Designed and built in sixteen years, seventeen thousand
Working-class families given turn-key homes with designs
Influenced by radical public-housing trends in Rotterdam.

Yet still you could never garner sufficient political backing
To alleviate slum conditions witnessed on your commute
From this modernist St Mobhi Road house build by Linzell:
A speculator as shrewd as his in-law, Alexandra Strain.

These builders prospered by focusing on the social caste
Who could afford the prestigious cachet of stained glass
And bay windows showcasing parlours kept for visitors.

During their annual smoking dinners in the Dolphin Hotel,
I wonder what such esteemed pillars of the Association
Of Dublin Housebuilders made of you, crippled by stress
At trying to build your parallel city for the dispossessed?
A foreigner in a city so scared of innovation or dissent
That this street you lived on underwent a name change
Amid protests at it being called after a Protestant dean.
It is unsurprising that no plaque here bears your name
That few remember. Our public acts of remembrance
Rarely commemorate workaday citizens who construct
Tangible legacies measureable in bricks and lime mortar.

So let me recall the last morning you opened this gate,
The explanatory note already folded in your pocket.
You cast a last look at St Mobhi Road before driving
Across this city you did more to shape than anyone.
Your mind plagued by all the tasks still to be done:
Delays on designated sites needing to be built on,
Families on waiting lists desperate for new homes.
Harassed faces of your depleted, overwhelmed staff,
Vacancies left unfilled, innumerable sets of plans
Constantly seeming to multiply, piled on your desk.

Paymasters had blocked your plans for more inner-city
Blocks of flats that families from adjacent tenements
Could be decanted into, leaving communities intact.
No more curved angles or such expressionist finesse
As befitted Corporation flats named after a countess.
No more oversailing eaves in the art deco complexes

You fantasised about, sharing a bed with four brothers.
Instead councillors insatiably demand the quick-fix
Of soulless sprawls of cheaply prefabricated estates.

As you drive, you recall awaiting a whistle in a trench;
Three decades later, the blasts of bombs still resonate.
Memories get muddled: amid the dead of no-man's-land
You see a guard signal to your father to release the brake
Of his huge hissing train, besieged by steam and smoke
On your ninth birthday, when he let you ride in his cab;
The stoker shovelling coal as if that heaving locomotive
Was a beast to be fed. This was the life you might have led
Had you not endured a war, unmentionable in Dublin,
That left you scarred by horrors never revealed to anyone.

Trying to shake those wartime blasts from your head,
You recall your father, one night during your boyhood,
Describe the damp misery of his first job as a shepherd.
You remember the sneers of fellow university students
At your pair of dilapidated boots worn for three years.
You feel guilty about the letters needing urgent replies
In the office you drive past on route to Dún Laoghaire.
There, you wander amid crowds, a condemned man
On day release, knowing the cell door will slam again;
Knowing that if you fight for sixteen more years to erect
Thousands of new homes, it still wouldn't be enough.

It has been four weeks now since you properly slept,
The black dog at your shoulder refusing any respite,
The beast who padded at your heels into an asylum
And pretended to retreat when fended off by tablets
You ceased taking when they interfered with your work.

But this morning you had finally ordered your thoughts,
Set out the helpless position, the impossible weight,
As clearly as in the days when, as a young draftsman,
You crafted every detail of your first architectural plan,
Discovering how a sanctuary existed in the parameters
Of blank sheets where you felt indubitably in command
Of the perspective, making every angle and aspect clear:
'I cannot stand it any longer, my brain is too tired to work.
It has not had a rest for twenty years except in heavy sleep.
Always on the go like a dynamo and still work is piled on me.
I am sorry to cause bother but think I am going slowly mad.'

You read your last words again, seated alone in your car
As dusk obscures the train tracks at Coal Quay Bridge.
Whiskey sours your stomach, but you take a final swig
Before opening the car door to walk over and observe
The neat symmetry of sleepers laid by railway workers.
Studying the lights of the ongoing train, you suddenly
Feel like a boy again, waiting for your father to come,
Driving his engine, the carriages filled with fallen men,
At top speed in his haste to get home to Kentish Town.
Patiently you await him by that unlit stretch of track,
Choosing your moment to step forth into the unknown.

The Street Photographer

In memory of Abraham Feldman,
also known as Arthur Fields

I

A homeless girl, crouched on a flattened cardboard box,
Now occupies your allotted spot, plastic cup held aloft
To crowds who cross this bridge with the same indifference
They showed towards you during that forlorn final decade
Of the half century during which you positioned yourself
In the path of the multitudes who traversed the Liffey
Amid busy lives, with only a diminishing trickle pausing,
Lured by your antiquated camera and a handwritten sign
That hung from your neck: *Instant colour photographs.*

Few passers-by knew your name, but you possessed two:
Abraham Feldman, the Jewish one you were born with
Not long after your family fled persecution in Ukraine,
And Arthur Fields, a more neutral pseudonym chosen
To allow you to blend into these adopted Dublin streets.
You and your brothers were living proof of how astute
Joyce was to make his fictitious refugee, Rudolf Virag,
Change the surname he bequeathed to his son to Bloom.

Joyce's Dublin was unalterable, yours never stayed still
As you chronicled it from opposite ends of the spectrum:
Joyce immortalising fleeting encounters, you discarding
Thousands of vignettes in every unsold negative destroyed;
Those photos with serial numbers that no punters came
To pay your wife to develop in a small darkroom located
In a side street.
                              But you accumulated enough ten shilling

Notes to raise a family from the curiosity of strangers
Who wanted mementos of Holy Communions or first dates,
Or a family seeing off a daughter onto an emigrant ship.
You provided evidence for people unable to afford cameras,
To let children recall how loved they were by grandparents
Who skimped for weeks to buy them confirmation dresses
Or take them into town to a proper café as a birthday treat.
While you and Bloom navigated insular cities, paradoxically
The two men whose eyes we now vividly see Dublin through
Were slighted outsiders, a Hungarian and a Ukrainian Jew.

Not that you had time to engage in philosophical musing,
Focused, like most émigrés, on the mechanics of making a living,
On gambits locals never considered, too fixed in their thinking.
Firstly, a sound studio for the inquisitive to record their voices,
Then you purchased a box camera to join the street photographers
Competing on O'Connell Street. You bagged one side of the
        bridge.
Your brother plied the same trade, hogging the other balustrade.

Elegant in your prime, your Ukrainian features radiated mystique,
Exuding glamour throughout the 1940s by attracting glamour
On nights when excited girls posed on route to dinner dances,
Beaus, awkward in dress suits, eager for your numbered card,
Lest the surprise gift of a photo might unlock amorous favours.
You were the closest Dubliners came to encountering paparazzi,
Momentarily allowed to star in the plotlines of their own lives,
Couples first snapped when courting and then with children,
Their lives chronicled in monochrome images in biscuit tins.

But cities change, technologies evolve, occupations disappear:
Gas lamplighters, shorthand typists, letterpress compositors.
By 1981, aged eighty, you became a relic from a bygone era

Who still felt compulsively compelled to stand on that bridge.
With your darkroom gone, you now sold instamatic Polaroids
That bled into colour when patiently held in your palm.
A seven-mile walk endured every morning, the same walk
When exhaustion or hunger made you abandon your post,
Footsteps slow, shoulders sagged, until, aged eighty-seven,
You took your final photograph, the first sold in weeks,
Of an Italian photographer who, seeing you, was transported
To the streets of his youth. He asked you to autograph it.
As if finally declining your parents' warnings to blend in,
You signed it, not in the name you lived by, but the name
They gave you after fleeing persecution: Abraham Feldman.

You died, aged ninety-three, leaving no archive behind,
Not expecting anyone outside your family to remember you.

II

Studying thousands of photographs that strangers kept,
I'm struck by how your art lay in its absence of art,
In opportunistic randomness, with no time for finesse
When you raised your camera. Yet you still possessed
An instinctive ability to frame each moment snatched
From the street life that evolved like a speeded-up film,
With you the only unalterable fixture on that bridge.
Your appearance changed from a flamboyant presence
Into resembling an old penitent condemned to repeat
The task of lifting your camera like an act of repentance,
Long after the world had ceased to need the services
Of street photographers to sell us back our own lives.

Your thoughts fascinate me, or maybe an absence of thought.
Did staring through a lens alleviate any other need to think?
You lived in a continuum, taking just enough care to frame
People you hadn't time to care about: punks sporting
    mohawks,
Tipsy civil servants allowed half an hour to cash pay cheques.
This became photography not as work but as ritual or fetish.
Not that dark secrets lay hidden among hoarded negatives
Because no negatives were hoarded, no image developed
If not already paid for. You looked into no person's soul,
Unless in the early years when certain sights were new
And you'd a brother on the opposite pavement to nod to
If movie stars passed or girls unaware of burgeoning beauty.
Did you both slip into the Yiddish that your parents spoke
As you joked about the preening foibles of passing folk
Or was your talk always about the tally of pictures sold?

Your separateness wasn't just from being at opposite ends
Of the lens from Dubliners, but from being unable to avail
Of their insular complacency throughout the Hitler conflict
When they accepted *Irish Press* assurances that nothing
Your fellow Jews endured in Poland was worse than injustices
Suffered by Ulster Catholics, while Irish papers castigated
Uninformed citizens who paid the Hitler war undue attention.
In June 1945 you watched couples leaving the Metropole,
Unwilling to meet your eye or pose for pictorial reminders
Of the night they were forced to leave a censored cocoon
Smugly woven around themselves and face harsh truths
Embedded into your DNA since your parents fled hatred.
People felt angry at those newsreels making them confront
Piled up skeletal bodies in Belsen, gaunt eyes of survivors

Staring from the screen while they shifted in discomfiture
In the Grand Circle's plush seats amid Corinthian columns,
Fearful to give credence to horrors beyond comprehension
Lest this acceptance saw them stigmatised as West Britons.

IV

Joyce claimed Dublin could be rebuilt from his masterpiece
But only gave us, in scrupulously indelible detail, one day.
The sole indelible detail in your Dublin was the balustrade
On O'Connell Bridge. Fashions changed before your lens.
You captured beehive hairstyles, bell-bottoms, rising hems,
Elephant flares, spandex skirts, ankle boots and tube-tops.
Any opinions on trends you kept to yourself as you stood,
Surrounded by such crowds that you resemble a boulder
Around which river water finds its way. You parted crowds
And stood apart in crowds. That is how I remember you
In my youth. No matter how packed that bridge became
You radiated a fixed solitude. You were there, yet not there,
In public solitary confinement, trapped within a migrant's
Compulsion to pay their way. Snapping all who stopped
Without truly seeing us or realising how your life's work
Was to chronicle a city that was home to Arthur Fields
But perhaps never to Abraham Feldman.
                                        It was left to strangers to select
What was preserved from your oeuvre. The random shots
That passers-by bought, sensing they would feel significant
When rediscovered years later in emptied out drawers.
Mementos of casual moments when we weren't dressed up
For formal occasions, presenting our best face to the world,
But were just being ourselves because it wasn't important,
It was a snap on a bridge, taken by chance and purchased
From curiosity. But maybe we were never so true to ourselves

70

Because we could see in your eyes how you didn't care, how
In many respects you were not truly there.
              This leads back to the undeveloped negative
Of your thoughts during those days spent in wind and rain,
When you aged but felt we always remained the same age.
Jorge Luis Borges would have much to say to you about life.
You'd have nothing to say to him; you said nothing to anyone,
Walking home every night to the wife who washed your hair
Before you slept to find strength to recommence your
    purgatory.
You missed her funeral, standing instead in your usual spot,
Perhaps knowing no way to express emotion or frame grief
Except through taking Polaroids that tried to freeze time.
But you out of time, a relic who plied an obsolete trade.

V

You professed no wish for remembrance, so the strange irony
Is how your pictures keep being unearthed to fill missing gaps
In many family histories. Often they exist with no real context
Or commentary, except perhaps a date scribbled on the back
To indicate that someone regarded this moment as precious
And kept your photo to remind them of a person they knew,
Or remind their descendants about the lives they once led,
Because these informal photographs, snapped by the man
On the bridge are often the only images of them that survive.
Our grandparents when so much younger than we are now,
Giddy in the adventure of love that brought us into being;
Nameless aunts who lost touch after emigrating to seek work
Or young best friends who swore to never forget each other
But died in nursing homes, having forgotten their own names.

The rich owned their Nikon Rangefinders and expensive Leicas.
They had lush photo albums and Bell and Howell cine cameras.
But you were our photographer, making us momentarily pause
When rushing to catch the last bus to Ballyfermot or Crumlin,
Amazed to find you still there in old age, still touting for trade,
Still in essence an émigré, yet so indelibly a part of our city
That you achieved the ultimate in fame, which is anonymity:
The man on the Bridge who never appeared in any photograph,
But became an ever-present witness, on the fringe of everything.

Matsuo Bashō in Mountjoy Prison

I
Beneath your moist tongue
That stirs memories of sex,
    A sim card's sharp edge.

II
Some nights my jail cell
Expands to depths only found
    In drugs or in Christ.

III
For practice I stare
At random bricks in my cell
    Until they blink first.

IV
Prism of dawn sky
Spilt by harbinger of joy:
    A drone that drops drugs.

V
I never slop out:
You must learn to hold your piss
    Like I hold my tongue.

VI
Few men really know
What they are doing in life.
    I'm doing eight years.

VII

I know I would steal
Sacred nails from the True Cross.
    Are you this honest?

VIII

Smells I miss of home:
My wife burns my shoes to turn
    Evidence to ash.

IX

My daughter visits,
Young breasts filling out her blouse.
    Wise lags look elsewhere.

X

Blades taped together:
Conflict resolution takes
    Its twin-track approach.

XI

A lag who needs more
Than seventeen syllables
    Is likely a snitch.

XII

You find true darkness
Not when screws turn off the lights.
    Look inside yourself.

XIII

I wake with a start.
The dark cell does not scare me:
    Just the dark within.

XIV

I don't miss the buzz
Of paid orgies after heists.
    I miss the walks home.

XV

My kids don't know me.
Jail lets me hide the imprint
    Left by my da's fists.

XVI

When my bullet comes
I'll feel cheapened if they send
    A cut-price greenhorn.

XVII

Grant me purgatory
To give me more time to kick
    The shit from my da.

XVIII

No purgatory waits.
Death will be a blank sentence
    With no remission.

My Eyes

My eyes weren't lying in wait when you chanced on them
At the padlocked gates of a Protestant church, so remote
That interments rarely discommode the slanting headstones

Or moss-choked gravel where I parked, invisible to anyone
Until they rounded the bend of that narrow country lane
Where I waited to collect a hiker after her Sunday walk.

I knew nothing of your bolthole cottage beyond the church,
With surveillance cameras arrayed on its fortified gates,
Where you retreated to brood on dead friends to avenge

And who might double-cross you during drug shipments.
I was unaware of your identity when we came face to face
After you braked hard on that bend, when spying me there.

The chilling coldness with which your eyes scrutinised mine,
Calculating risk, gauging dangers to which I was oblivious,
Thinking you were just a big swinging dick young executive

Annoyed to find someone occupying a favoured parking space.
Revving your engine, you passed with a contemptuous glare,
Dismissing me as too inconsequential to pose any threat.

Two weeks later, I recalled your stare, watching news footage
Of that church cordoned off, your windscreen shattered,
An assassin's car burnt out in the spot where I had parked.

I still wake some nights and wonder if, when taken by surprise
By that waiting car, your final thought was a fervent prayer
To glimpse me there, your saviour with inconsequential eyes.

A Poet of the 1970s

In the end everything he laboured on was left unresolved:
His valedictory novel missing its unforgettable epilogue,

The soliloquy to end his final play suspended in mid-flow,
The questions plaguing his work seemingly unanswerable.

Years later, if any of his colleagues were asked to recall
This affable unassuming companion, briefly famous

For the number of times he seemed destined for fame,
Their final memories all contained a disconcerting sense

That the slouch of his shoulders receding in the distance
Resembled a question mark seeking the end of his sentence.

The Slant

Gradually he came to realise that the answer
To life's riddle was that life possessed no riddle,
The actuality of living was complicated only
By his habit of overcomplicating it for himself.
A habit ingrained after his innocence got stolen

At eight years old, lured into unsettling games
In a neighbour's car, then sworn to secrecy
And sent veering off in a skewed elliptical orbit,
Bewildered by what occurred, robbed of the buoyancy
And bearings that other children instinctively possess.

He wakes, perturbed by what left him unperturbed
Throughout the half century he put it out of his head.
But that theft has remained lodged there, a cloud
He was barely conscious of, too busy bustling about,
Trying to flee its shadow, assuring himself he was fine

So often he grew to believe it, preoccupied by the riddle
Of why life felt so complex, why the earth seemed to lean
At a curious slant that makes a street look unbalanced
When a child flees from a car, perplexed, gazing askance
At rows of familiar terraces succumbing to subsidence.

Making Things Happen

For Marian Fitzpatrick and Tina Robinson

Things don't happen: things are made to happen
By those people who choose to remain unseen;

By people who look at a boarded-up building
And re-envisage it as a brimming theatre;

Who gaze at a loose configuration of streets
And see them come together as a village;

Whose names never feature in the headlines,
Being neither seekers of attention or acclaim,

But whose intuition concurs with Leopold Bloom's
That revolutions occur on the due instalments plan.

If it is true that Balthasar, Melchior and Caspar
Did arrive, anxious to brandish flashy gifts

Of gold, myrrh and frankincense, it is only because
Someone behind the scene possessed the sense

To saddle camels and point out exactly which star
To follow, someone made that epic voyage feasible,

Then retreated to the margins, far too immersed
In making new things happen to take a curtain call

At the encore, when kings theatrically bow their heads
In a stable, having only somehow made it there on time

Because unobtrusive gods flitted through the cosmos,
Orchestrating the darkness to let that star shine.

The Town Carried in his Head
In honour of Piet Chielens

Joyce boasted of how his Dublin could be rebuilt,
Brick by brick, by some future reader of *Ulysses*.
However no necessity arose to rebuild his city.
It simply evolved or decayed, reshaped by tides
Of redevelopments and recessions, to resemble
A succession of imprints from one fraying stamp.

But to walk the streets of Ieper with Piet Chielens
Is like seeing a town perpetually reassemble itself
In multitudinous maps, simultaneously overlaid,
Layer upon layer, transposed in the mind of a man
Immersed in the immediacy of the here and now,
The everyday joys and tragedies of life around him.

His days of overseeing exhibitions in a museum
Or helping strangers locate a lost relative's grave
Are followed by the quietude of evenings spent
With loved ones and friends.
                              Perpetually conscious of how
These everyday benedictions of domestic life play out
On streets where ghosts have squatters' rights to occupy
Each rebuilt pavement, each formerly decimated dwelling,
Roads once so cratered and flooded that no landmarks
Existed to allow men to formulate any true coordinates,
To pinpoint the spot where their limbs got blown asunder
Or they saw boys, too young to shave, suffocated in mud.

This duality is inherent in being born in what was once
A salient of horror, slaughterously taken and retaken.
But after the armistice it stole back its original identity

As a rural latticework of deelgemeentes, quiet communes
Filled with merchants, weavers, breweries, tilled acres,
Its serenity only broken by keenly contested cycling races.
Two heritages: one imposed by visitors keen to preserve
This salient as the shrine of remembrance, frozen in time;
The other in which locals got on with the actualities of life,
Immune to a backdrop of cemeteries dotting their horizon.

Flanders is no mere landscape of battle sites. It breathes
With every new life started here, grieves every local death
From old age or cancer or accidental intrusions of the past;
A farmer burning stubble on the day, when after decades
Of torturously inching its way up to the surface, a live shell
Killed him after he had peacefully tilled this field all his life.

Piet, it would have been easier to forget the tangled legacy
Of foreign armies who fought here, leaving behind the dead
They could bury and multitudinous thousands more still missing.
You could have been an architect, a university professor,
A genial entrepreneur welcoming patrons to his emporium.
You could have ignored the miasma lingering in dawn mist
Over these graves; instead you tried to diffuse it with music,
Tasking yourself to shoulder that weight of remembrance.

Visitors stand nightly for the Last Post at the Menin Gate
But you can visualise when grass banks marked this gap
In the ramparts that once led to a bridge over the moat.
You can name the first family killed, sheltering in a cellar
Of the inn located there, back when the town's inhabitants
Couldn't envisage the devastation of those artillery shells.

Your history isn't about military alliances calculated to serve
Empires scheming to subdivide colonies or recalibrate power.

It declines to glorify blood-soaked chess played by generals.
It involves the reclamation of family stories cut short
In entwining circles of hell, labyrinths offering no escape,
With bodies hastily buried where they fell or sucked beneath
Quagmires of mud, with scant chance of being recovered.
Yet someone like you can carry a loom inside your mind
Where you interweave the names of the missing with dates
When their brigades lost men crossing every perch of land.

Now when foundations are dug for roads or industrial units,
Shattered bones are still found, fragmented clues unearthed
That might finally yield up the identity of some young man
Who died in a place inalienably foreign to any he ever knew.
You have spent years at excavations and belated autopsies,
Patiently trying to piece together whatever can be gleaned
From buttons or frayed threads of what was once a uniform.
All that matters in your battles is the common humanity
Of combatants from fifty nations whose lives ended here;
A man's rank no longer counts, nor whether he was French,
German or Indian, British or Irish, Australian or Austrian.

You bring to this task decades of study and compassion,
Straining to reunite a man with his name. You cannot see
Their faces but can sense the overwhelming stench of fear
From boys not just bewildered to have been here in life
But to be left in limbo, leading subterranean non-existences
Beneath fields and roadways, factories and the neat homes
Of people who truly call this place home. The neighbours
You walk among after your work at the museum is done,
Greeted by acquaintances as you stroll, growing immersed
In their latest news, in the minutiae of regional politics,
The pertinent issues forming the tapestry of contemporary life

To which you are integral, pausing to talk at pavement cafés,
Swapping opinions with fellow shoppers queuing for bread.

Yet at times, stepping back onto the street, you find yourself
Walking amid ghosts that are still waiting to be found.
Going home to loved ones, you retrace their steps again,
Disinterested in their motives, only in the common bond
Of men ensnared in a nightmare few could comprehend,
When facing death on what is now a quiet street corner,
Wondering if, in later years, anyone would remember them.
Not as statistics or symbols or recruiting propaganda fodder,
But as part of the story of a town that existed before them
And exists a century after a random shot claimed their lives,
With some screaming for their mothers or others for Christ,
But few imagining how the fullest remembrance would come,
From a contemplative local, quietly going about his life,
Cognisant that the present is built on the weight of the past.

Civil War

The bitterest of Civil Wars are fought in silence.
Two former friends who passed each other daily
For half a century with only the curtest of nods;

The barest acknowledgement of a secret shared,
Of a battle, never spoken about, that was fought
In two confrontations on each woman's doorstep,

With neither inviting their neighbour to come in.
The first, a knock followed by accusations about
One of their sons having got a daughter pregnant.

This accusation countered with defensive retorts
By his mother who cried after slamming her door.
Eight months later, she rang her neighbour's bell

With no words exchanged, but a gleaming new pram
Left on the step without admission of responsibility,
But the sense of duty discharged, honour satisfied

Between two matriarchs. The child grow up mystified
By why he never saw his gran and the kind neighbour,
Who secretly gave him sweets, exchange a single word.

Men as Old as the Century

In November 1989, she makes the long trek from Lusk,
Navigating bottleneck roundabouts that necklace Swords
As she listens to radio reports about young East Germans
Overwhelming perplexed guards to scale the Berlin Wall
And splinter it with pickaxes, while crowds on the far side
Cheer, holding aloft champagne and flowers in welcome.

This news blares from a television in the geriatric ward
Where her uncle nods as she enters, unsure of who she is
But sufficiently cognisant to recognise her as the crew-cut
Woman who smuggles him in whiskey twice every week.
They watch the news, but she is unsure what he takes in:
This man, as old as the century, surrounded by elderly
Local men, with memories disappearing into dementia.

It takes a moment to realise that a question, fiercely
Repeated by a patient in the next bed, is directed to her:
'*How did you get here, boy?*' Aware how men on this ward
Are always alert for any chance to cadge a lift to return
To the former homes where they were unable to cope alone,
She pretends she has no car and replies, '*I came by bus.*'

The man glares at her, his tone angry, gaze incredulous.
'*By bus? What bucking eejit comes to Loughshinny by bus?*
Where in God's name did you even lay your hands on one
At this hour of night, boy, and for a job as secret as this?
Blast you anyway if you blow the cover of the rest of us.'
Her uncle stares ahead, as if he cannot hear this tirade

Or has heard it too many times, marooned in that ward
Where, after admission, men know they will never leave;
That is, if by then, they even know their own name or age.

Some patients retreat to silence, others revert to childhood,
Eyesight blurred by glaucoma or eclipsed by cataracts.
But this old man's eyes blaze with a frenetic passion
As if whatever recurring memory he is trapped within
Is the sole remaining recollection that still feels real.
His gaze never wavers. It creates a disconcerting sense
That his body is possessed by a young ghost of himself,
A youth alert to every sound and source of danger,
Someone who cannot see her in this geriatric ward,
As he stares through her at the spectres in his head.
'Are you one of the Mooretown lads brought by Finn?
Or the Balbriggan lads Michael Lynch promised us?
Either way, you're a blasted fool not to come by bike,
So expect no lift on my crossbar when this coastline
Is ablaze, from Rogerstown all the way out to Rush.
I barely slept a wink last night, going over every plan,
Phone lines to cut, petrol and paraffin requisitioned,
Everything that needs doing or that could go wrong.
After tonight, the whole shebang is out of our hands,
But if the guns get smuggled on that New York ship,
We'll have every coast guard station burnt by dawn
So no prying eyes will spy us bringing them ashore.'

His eyes close in exhaustion, his breathing laboured.
Other patients too absorbed in private worlds to pay heed,
Nurses and orderlies too immersed in doing their work.
When he reawakens she knows he'll have no memory
Of having addressed her and no clue as to where he is.

What will he see when looking around? Wooden bunks
In Ballykinlar Internment Camp? Balbriggan's streets
In smouldering ruins? Terrified horses all whinnying
When the IRA burnt an army remount station in Lusk?
The sight of Jack McCann's body lying on the roadway
After British forces dragged him from his house in Rush?
Or will this man wake trapped in other sets of memories,
From the jumble of decades since that night when he felt
As exultant as the young East Germans now on the news
That her uncle fixatedly stares at, ignoring her presence
And that of the agitated man asleep in the adjoining bed.

Then she wonders if perhaps her uncle does know him?
Maybe – even in this ward where memories keep receding
Like a tide on Balcarrick beach that never comes back in –
During a rare lucid moment her uncle has recognised him
As a youth with whom he once sheltered near a boathouse,
Awaiting a signal to smash down a coast guard station door,
Assuring the occupants they meant their families no harm
And even helping them to gather up personal possessions.
Suitcases packed within minutes, furniture shifted outside,
Bewildered children harried from beds to huddle forlornly
In the dark, saying farewell to the only homes they knew,
As paraffin got sprinkled throughout the family quarters
To ensure that nobody occupied these outposts again.

Because she knows of this night the man keeps reliving,
When the North County Dublin coast was lit by flames
From six coast guard stations simultaneously set alight,
With families who lived in those dwellings made homeless
After Michael Collins sent word of guns to be landed there.
Old naval officers given minutes to gather their belongings
Before being told to walk in the dark away from the blaze,

Aware they were now too tainted to find local work again.
The IRA units fleeing by bicycle or commandeering cars,
Aware that the road to Loughshinny would soon swarm
With auxiliaries roused from their camp in Gormanston
To clamber from Crossley tenders and initiate terror,
Though finding their threats met by a code of Omertà.

Had the man in this bed been among those volunteers
Or was this a tale told to him by someone who was there
But which, in his confusion, he now mistook as his own?
Either way, amid the mayhem within his capsizing brain,
This memory, whether true or false, is all he can cling to,
More real than this ward where time has lost all meaning.

Did he ever openly discuss that raid during the decades
That followed the Truce, declared a mere sixteen days
After those families were rendered homeless, its terms
Already being secretly negotiated, although the men
Risking their lives to attack those coast guard stations
Were no more aware of this than they were of the fact
That their arms shipment was impounded in New York.
Therefore this night was not the apex of their struggle,
But presaged the moment when actuality intervened,
With simple camaraderie being an insufficient bulwark
When aspirations needed to acquire a quantifiable form.

Maybe for this man the trauma of those years became
Something only spoken about among trusted friends
Or never mentioned at all. Just like her uncle rarely spoke
About the elation he and his comrades must have felt
On the night when they saw the coast being set alight,
And paused, mid-flight, to savour the same exhilaration
Displayed by young East Germans on the Berlin Wall,

Content for now to exalt in their moment of triumph,
And leave all questions about the future for the future.
The news coverage switches to other euphoric crowds
Thronging streets in Czechoslovakia and Yugoslavia;
Showing a shared joy felt in Srebrenica and Sarajevo,
As people watch an empire of Soviet influence crumble,
And savour a new freedom where nothing can go wrong.

Her uncle has never openly talked about those times,
The only hint of old allegiances or grievances evident
In which neighbours he nodded to, while other men
Were passed by without a hint of acknowledgement.
She suspects he has secrets he wants buried with him.
She has seen this courteous bachelor turn waspish
If her siblings probe too much. There are old medals
Remaining mute in a bedroom drawer. She has seen
Nights when he sat up late, brooding over whiskey.
As is the way with men who have known real fighting,
He stays silent about some things he must have seen.

There are only two nights he has ever spoken about,
Unexpectedly, driving his egg van down a back road
Where a landmark provoked a vivid memory, so that
Suddenly she barely knew him, his voice so different,
Like he was nineteen again, simultaneously fearless
And petrified, describing that night when the coast
Was ablaze, and everything felt exhilaratingly possible,
As if that conflagration had shifted the earth on its axis
So that nothing could ever possibly be the same again,
And there was no thought of future disunity or factions
Because everyone felt intoxicated by the song they sang.

The old man in the next bed interrupts her thoughts,
His eyes reopen, as if seeing her for the first time,
Tone belligerent as he asks, '*How did you get here, boy*?'
She can no more engage him in any true conversation
Than talk to this uncle, unaware she is his next of kin.
She cannot fill the missing gaps in what they remember
Or ask either man if he recalls the other man being there
On the night they lit fires to blind the eyes of an empire.

She will never know if these two men had a friendship
Destroyed by schisms and bitterness in the Civil War,
Or if, when it ended, this man was among the winners
Enjoying state posts or an Irish Sweepstakes sinecure,
Or whether he spent a half century as a farm labourer.
Here in this ward he doesn't know his life story either,
Having mentally retreated to his early impetuous days
Before freedom became something requiring definition,
When it was an aspiration that hung lightly in the air,
With nights filled with dangers to be willingly withstood,
And nobody had words for the stress they endured.

Had this man been among the volunteers like her uncle
Present in Portrane asylum when one of Collins's Squad
Of elite hitmen suddenly went berserk at a dance there,
Being held in a padded cell that he slashed with a knife
Until senior Squad gunmen were summoned from Dublin
To try and calm his nerves. This is the only other night
Her uncle has ever mentioned; local volunteers trying
To make light of what we call post-traumatic stress,
Telling him his pent-up madness was just whiskey talk
And he would be grand after some air on the cliff walk
Where they sat on the rocks to let him recover his wits,
Watching him stare out to sea with the expectant gaze

That her uncle surely once possessed, when standing
Beside the burnt coast guard station, waiting in vain,
Night after night, for intercepted guns that never came.

Joseph Mary Plunkett's Rosary Beads

Just for once let a poem be not about him, but about me;
William Hand, who never saw my twenty-third birthday,
Being destined for annihilation amid the slaughter at Arras.

But, aged twenty, I shivered in Kilmainham Jail at dawn,
A bit-player centurion used to flesh out a crucifixion scene,
Bewildered to have landed in Dublin instead of France.

Perhaps the watching padre thought I had the upper hand,
My rifle quivering among others in that jittery firing squad,
But, awaiting the order, I knew nobody would remember me.

The prisoner sensed it too, his neck swathed in bandages
From some tubercular ailment, his gaunt skin so pallid
We wondered if he had enough strength to cross that yard.

Yet he strode with composed eloquence to his appointed spot,
Displaying no fear or hostility as he appraised our faces
And then unexpectedly offered me his rosary beads as a gift

In a benign gesture of kinship. It felt like an invitation
To be a footnote in a rebellion I knew nothing about;
A trembling soldier, trying my best to aim at his heart

For his sake, unsure if my chamber contained the live round
That felled a bridegroom who was wed under military escort
In the freezing prison chapel seven hours before being shot.

Such an eerie feeling to walk away with ivory rosary beads,
Still warm from his fingers, tucked into my tunic pocket
Beside my small service book, with its edicts of army rules

And regulation form for me to fill out the details of my will.
I sensed, as I left him slumped in the stone breakers' yard,
That I was being quick marched towards an abyss of oblivion,

A piece of cheap meat awaiting my turn to be dispatched
To whatever hellhole best served the needs of my superiors.

I resolved to leave his ivory beads with my cousin, Dora,
In case, like me, they would get lost amid the quagmire

That swallowed me up after two more years of fighting.
When the telegram boy knocked at 6, Piccadilly Cottages,

In Derbyshire, I wanted these beads to serve as proof that,
Like my victim destined for immortality, I too had an existence

Before I drew the short straw, allowing a sniper time to aim
By accepting a third light from the same match lit in a trench.

*William Hand of Derbyshire was a member of the firing
squad who executed the poet Joseph Mary Plunkett at 3.47
a.m. on 4 May 1916, following the 1916 Rising. Hand was
killed in France in 1918. Decades later, his cousin Dora
presented Plunkett's rosary beads to the National Museum of
Ireland. For decades after the First World War, old soldiers
from the trenches remained superstitious about allowing
their cigarette to be the third one lit from the same match.*

After Grace

Cinemagoers enter the Metropole at random times
During continuous screenings in this picture palace,
Rebuilt in such splendour that now the sole reminder
Of how O'Connell Street was once a smouldering shell
Is my presence, dining alone as always, in the modest
Café located off the foyer, barely visible to the couples
Chattering excitedly before they enter the auditorium.

Not that many recognise me, if they bothered to look,
Though few people glance at solitary women my age.
When some do, I sense them struggle to reconcile my face
With that tragic figure, as they prefer to envisage me,
Being led down gas-lit prison corridors, a bride-to-be,
Destined to become a widow just seven hours later.

I was striking looking then, ashen-faced for many reasons,
Though determined not to let the soldiers with bayonets
Watching in that prison chapel see how I inwardly shook,
When allotted my place at the altar as they led in my Joseph
And, for a few minutes, an officer removed his handcuffs.
Seeing him, I felt like Elizabeth, mother of John the Baptist,
Who, hearing Mary's voice, felt the babe leaping in her womb.
We had so much to say, but we were denied privacy to say it.
Not even the chaplain's voice conjured a sense of intimacy
As we exchanged vows. Then Joe was led away, handcuffed,
And I had to wait amid those grey cells I later came to know,
Until an officer condescended to grant us a final ten minutes;
Our every gesture scrutinised, every stilted word overheard
By soldiers crowding his cell, tasked to escort me away
To let them commence the procedures for his execution.

Sometimes in dreams I cradle our stillborn child and ask
If she was the Rising's final victim? Thomas Clarke's wife
Also miscarried, in such anguish she could barely speak,
But at least, in time, she could refer to it, have her grief
Publically acknowledged, openly mourn that heartache
Amid her other losses. My grief needed to remain private
Although after Joe's death I possessed no private space,
No door I might close and truly call some room my home.
I was like a catkin blown about at the breeze's mercy,
My mother disdainfully condemning me to journalists
In her autocratic cut-glass Protestant Dublin accent
As a headstrong girl with whom she had severed all ties.
My mother-in-law begrudgingly found me a space
Among her myriad properties that raked in sufficient rent
To keep her adult children tied to her purse strings;
A landlady so fiercely tyrannical that when Joseph
Tried to give Jim Larkin money during the Lockout
The union leader denounced its source as too tainted.

Not that Joe's mother didn't endure her own heartache –
One son executed, two more jailed with her husband –
But insurrection was more acceptable than a scandal,
Especially if involving a son seen as a Catholic martyr.
For seven hours I played a walk-on part in her family.
But with Joe gone, I was an intruder and a convert
With too much Protestant blood not to be suspect
To a family who prudently acquired an august Papal title
To cement their status in the shifting social hierarchy.
Their servants watched me as closely as the soldiers
Who once denied me space to properly bid Joe farewell.
When I told them I felt unwell and asked to be left alone
His sister came to the doorway of my allotted room
And saw my chamber pot awash with foetus and blood.

We neither spoke, knowing there was nothing to be said.
She closed the door in a way that made it understood
That what we were witnesses to had never occurred.
Anything more that needed saying was said by solicitors
For Joseph's family who, for thirty contentious years,
While prepared to recognise his blood upon the rose
And in the stars the glory of his eyes, were still loath
To let themselves recognise his signature on the will
In which Joe valiantly tried to provide for his bride,
Who, to his family's irritation, refused to back down,
Like some cowed tenant they could serve notice on.

However nobody here in this foyer wishes to hear about
The fraught aftershock of a tragic midnight marriage.
People want stories about Joseph's flamboyant jewellery
And how I wear the ring a soldier tried to steal from him,
Tales of his courage, leaving a sick bed, neck swathed
In bandages after surgery, to fight not only an empire
But against the pleurisy and glandular tuberculosis
That left him infirm, yet still a dervish of nervous energy,
Striding forth in a uniform that he designed for himself
To befit what he perceived as a crusade for Ireland's soul.

Nobody wants to dwell on the fate of incidental victims,
But when I close my eyes I can see my sister Muriel,
The most frail and domesticated of us Gifford girls.
Like me, she married one of the poets they shot,
But was not allowed to see him before his execution.
Her nerves frayed, even before soldiers machine-gunned
Her house to render it uninhabitable. Left homeless,
She struggled in penury to mind two small children
Amid such grief that she could find no equilibrium.
Releasing her five-year-old's hand for one moment

At the top of a staircase in the department store
Where they were sent to have a photograph taken,
She watched him fall so badly he was hospitalised.
She never wanted to go on that holiday for families
Of the executed men. Defiant widows staked claim
To a stretch of beach in Skerries, where my sister
Left her daughter playing with shells. Muriel swam
Ever further out into the tide until her strength
And grieving heart simply gave out. Her son,
Left crippled by his fall, watched from a window
In the hospital as his mother's cortege went past,
Fourteen months after his father had been shot.

But few songs will be spun from such a sad story,
Suicide being as stigmatised as my pregnancy,
Both insufficiently heroic to further any cause.
Nobody wants to recall two sets of grandparents
Seeking custody of her orphaned children, a clash
Between two different religions and social castes,
Until Mama, who disinherited me, lost her case
To raise Muriel's children in closeted probity.

Family histories are too problematically complex
To ever be shoehorned into a neat narrative.
Before I became frozen in history as a tragic bride
I earned a living as an artist. Even today I sell
An occasional sketch or a magazine illustration
To supplement what meagre income I possess
After hounding pension boards to seek redress,
Unafraid to be obstinate and invoke Joe's name,
Reserving my right to vent fury or complain about
Which veterans grew enriched or were impoverished
In the decades after when it transpired that people

On this rebuilt street were more interested in jazz
Than in the Gaelic ideals Joe envisaged for them.

My instinct to sketch and draw has never dried up,
But it is more and more thwarted by the arthritis
That colonised my fingers during months in a cell
In that same prison where my husband was shot.
My jailers were men who fought alongside him
Seven years previously, during one glorious week
When whatever shape freedom was meant to take
Remained an abstraction no one needed to clarify:
When Joe – harbouring dreams that a new Ireland
Might invite a German prince to become our king –
Took his turn to tenderly carry the stretcher
Of James Connolly, with O'Connell Street in flames,
Aware that his wounded friend was a syndicalist
Fighting for a different vision of a socialist republic,
And that, if by fluke, their rebellion succeeded,
Then one friend would need to shoot the other.

I put down my cutlery, having finished my meal,
Anxious to be gone before the feature film ends
And bustling crowds of happy couples descend
The thickly carpeted stairs, excitedly extolling
The allure of Vivien Leigh or Katharine Hepburn.
I rarely attend movies now, partly out of poverty –
Though usherettes would discreetly wave me in –
But mainly because I prefer the films that play
In my mind. I come here to dine and be alone
Among crowds, instead of alone in the small flats
I flit between, based on where rent is affordable.
If I let John Ford direct a film about my life
People would adore seeing it enacted on screen,

Able to safely immerse themselves in my story,
While remaining detached from its aftermath
In which, most days, a widow dines on her own
After decades alone, as a consequence of the volley
That felled her husband and knocked her life off-kilter.
Here in this state I am meant to exist as a symbol
Of heroic sacrifice, not as a woman with opinions,
But I stubbornly occupy this space I have created
Where I let myself simply be myself. I pay my bill
And walk out of the foyer, unnoticed by anyone,
Into an O'Connell Street packed with window shoppers,
With cajoling street photographers, with corner boys
Lounging against the rebuilt GPO walls, with girls
Excitedly waiting for their dates under Clerys clock
In this city that pays me no heed as I walk alone,
Because, while I still remain inconveniently alive,
Nobody can condense my life into a sentimental song.

IV

An Evening Walk

1. The Gift of Boredom

Pedants may gloss it up as inspiration.
But we who walk neon-lit thoroughfares

Know the nature of the unconscious gift
That stealthily waylays our inattentiveness

To create white spray amid which poems come
Drifting towards us on the tides of boredom.

2. Eden Terrace

For my son, Diarmuid

While no Champs-Élysées, Las Ramblas or Alexanderplatz,
Surely this tiny cul-de-sac deserves a laudatory verse.
Hidden by steep steps that prevent vehicular access,

Its quartet of small single-storey cottages face each other.
A square so unobtrusively concealed for twelve decades
That passers-by are rarely ever aware of its existence,

Or how a boy longed to live here for its magical address
Or winters when newcomers found its name an apt choice,
Haven-seekers climbing its steps to catch a view of paradise.

3. An Empty Laneway

I have no idea if this lane ever possessed a name
Although for fifty years I've used it as a short cut,
Just to sense a subconscious echo of my excitement

As a boy leaving a bus to join bustling match-goers
Descending its steps in a rush to reach the stadium.

Back then it was only busy in the hour before kick-off.
Now – with match-day crowds gone – it is disturbed

Only by occasional footsteps: an old man walking his dog
Or a moocher seeing what can be scrounged from a skip

When building work is done on a house backing onto it.
Yet I still find myself going out of my way to cut down

This nameless unloved route, blighted by dock leaves,
Just to re-experience that boyish surge of anticipation.

Is this locked memory why I have always loved laneways,
For their barely noticeable but mysterious possibilities,

For how their insignificance still proffers the off chance
Of stumbling onto a vista that makes us stand entranced.

4. The Stammer

Workmen have cleared the overgrown riverbank
But no trace remains of their labour in this park

Except for one hacked fragment of a tree trunk
That got swept past the bridge and playground

To become entrapped beneath the small waterfall
Where a downstream current confronts an eddy

Of recirculating water that flows back over itself.
For days it has been pinned in this siphon grip,

Causing a dull thud every time it bashes the wall
And bobs beneath the weight of cascading water,

Like a soul in limbo, or like how I felt in childhood,
A stammering boy stuck on some unutterable word.

5. The Park

Panting slightly to crest the slope to the park gates
The man realised such joy was finite. A day would come

That was destined to be the last time he ever strolled
In this park he had casually traversed since boyhood.

Would he recognise the magnitude of that final walk?
Or would the evening feel the same as any excursion,

Remarkable only for how the incline felt steeper,
The noise of the playing children somehow fainter,

As he grew conscious of a tightness within his chest
That barely registered, like a distant house alarm

He was too busy catching his breath to bother with;
Too distracted in observing how a sunburst of light

Illuminated the gates so that the entwined sycamores
That framed his exit formed an exquisite curvature

Of dappled leaves; an archway conjuring a picture
Of guests forming an honour guard at a church door

To let newly-weds stoop beneath a tunnel of hands,
Eagerly racing to embrace whatever fate lay in store.

6. Pessoa Walks Through Dublin

When passing certain houses I recall their tragedies
During nightly *flânerie* to perambulate and speculate,

Observe and reflect. I've strolled long enough to accumulate
Secret histories, to decode signs no one else can decipher.

Like this plastic flower in the window of an ivy-clad villa
Into which a father moved his family, blissfully unaware

How within months he would be diagnosed with cancer.
I saw his ten-year-old tape this flower to the glass pane

On the night of his funeral, needing to make some gesture,
Leave some signal to let his soul know he was welcome,

A secret sign to be decrypted only by her deceased father.
Its petals symbolising hope until their meaning got lost

In the whorl of years when she grew so immersed in life
That she forgot why she attached it to this sash window,

Where it remains to this day; its providence so obscure
That others within her family seem reluctant to remove it.

I wonder if she remembers the night she taped it there
And stood in anguished silence, head bent in prayer,

Unaware of being observed by a *flâneur* walking his dog,
The stranger whom her father outbid for that residence,

The stroller who still recalls, on my walks up this street,
A girl framed at a lit window, distraught by his absence.

7. A Poem for Patricia Lynch
Author of The Turf Cutter's Donkey, *1894-1972*

It required a pandemic to make this birdsong
Sound as vibrant here as when greenfinches sang
In fields that once besieged this secluded road
Where you quietly wrote books for four decades.

You are almost forgotten now, but I still pause
To gaze at what was once your book-filled abode.
Your garden a riot of flowers, a weekly shopping list
Of sensible provisions phoned into Findlater & Co.
To arrive in late afternoon, after you finished writing
And patiently answered letters from young readers,
Whose parents were blithely unaware that you first
Came to Dublin to write reports for Sylvia Pankhurst's
Staunch communist paper, *The Workers' Dreadnought*,
Or how your husband, R.M. Fox, was upstairs typing
Defiant books about Lenin, Mao Zedong and Larkin.

During the lockdown birdsong was often the only sound
On this street as children learnt new lexicons of danger:
Infection rates, social distancing, phased reopening;
Phrases becoming as woven into their consciousness
As your book titles were for generations who adored
The Bookshop on the Quay or *The Old Black Sea Chest*.

No plaque exists, but you might feel embarrassed
By fuss in this deluxe enclave where you struggled
In old age; your husband gone, your novels starting
To drift out of print, your garden unmanageable
With your arthritic hands. Cocoa and cherry brandy

Became occasional treats that steered you to sleep,
As your house, unchanged since 1934, fell apart.
The modernist suntrap rooms, where you embarked
On fictional voyages, started to ship water and capsize,
Until a puppeteering family recognised your loneliness
And bestowed a miraculous final chapter to your life.

So perhaps it was apt, amid the birdsong of lockdown,
That while no physical hint of your presence pervaded
This street that felt as hushed as in any ghostly tale,
Sometimes I possessed an eerie sense, passing parked
Audi SUVs, sensible second cars and E-class Mercs.
I knew that this sensation of being watched was illusory
But often felt reluctant to look back in case I glimpsed
A turf cutter's donkey patiently standing on The Rise,
Its reins held by a spirited young girl and her brother,
While an old lady in a headscarf beckoned them forth
From this street where they were conjured into being
By a writer, robbed of all sense of home in childhood,
Who rediscovered it here with the man who loved her.

V

A New Life

Yellow Fields of Anastasia

I bore witness to – but knew I could never grasp –
The true depths of pain you were unable to hide
From visitors during months of convalescence,
When I needed to conceal from you my distress,
My pain and overwhelmed sense of helplessness
Every evening when I entered the hospital gates
To traverse yellow fields of Anastasia rapeseed
And park at a derelict red-oxide painted barn,
Aware you were awaiting my arrival, inconsolable
And overwrought, in tears I felt powerless to stem.

Your anguish tore at my heart. I had to brace myself
And feign strength to help you walk a few extra steps.
It seemed impossible for us to imagine any pain worse
Than that glacial pharmaceutical purgatory in there,
With you forced to drift anchorless, no shore in sight,
While I cried afterwards in my car, alone in the dusk,
Afraid to drive until palpitations eased in my chest.

Yet even amidst our shared and separate agonies,
I could imagine a pain deeper than any distress
That might greet me on my visits to that hospital,
Deeper than your despondency or my helplessness.
It was the loneliness that I would have endured,
My devastation, had you not been awaiting my arrival
At the end of that drive through the swaying stems
Of yellow Anastasia that shielded you from the world,
Till you felt able to stride unaided through fields again.

Music in My Golden Years

Back when I naively imagined myself
To be an indefatigable young virtuoso,
I'd have lacked the sixth sense to play
Such an elegant beautiful body as yours
At pianississimo pace, to patiently coax

And cajole these rippling grace notes.
It is an instrument too subtly strung
For a novice, bereft of any experience,
To cloak their lack of finesse behind
Blunt showboating feats of stamina;

Feeling they need to manically conduct
A vast symphony orchestra, grinding
Relentlessly on to the high-octane finale
Of a bombastic composition, rustled up
To impress bewigged Viennese despots.

It took me threescore years to discover
How equally sweet notes can be conjured
By even just blowing on one unfurled leaf
With slow precision and intuitive fingering,
Feeling no need to overwhelm with strength

As a lingering sigh is induced, soft enough
To render all musical notation superfluous.
A cry so pure that the poised percussionists
Pack their instruments and retreat off stage;

The horn section withdraws, with cellists
And contrabassoons rendered redundant;
The orchestra pit empties, the auditorium
Silent except for a trill from the upmost tier.

A quaver so secretive it can only be released
By an old soloist, not as good as he was once
But as good once as he ever was, strumming
Notes he has only learnt to summon with age.

Your True Height

I would equally love the other four inches of you:
The inches that forgot to grow in the aftershock

Of your father's death when you were only ten,
That stayed stum during subsequent upheavals
And mishaps, amidst the tragedies and trauma

You needed to navigate, at times with kindly help
But often as a child who found herself alone,
Needing to grow up so fast, forced to cope

With such adult responsibilities as a teenager
That the languid limbs you expected to inherit
Became stymied, bones stunted by stage fright.

But your extra four inches inhabit my dreams
At night, where, when you walk through them,
I see you approach as a figure of equal height.

Often you walk amid faces I cannot recognise,
Who died years before I came to be blessed
By having you enter my life from their world

In which they cared for you as best they could
With an abundance of love. They nod to me
On the unlit fringes of my unconsciousness,

Then step back, bidding farewell as you stroll
Beyond them into this life you made for yourself.
I wish I knew them or they knew of my gratitude

At what their love conjured: David and June.
We never speak but I sense how they also sense
That, in your sleeping state, you blossom forth

By those four inches only they and I can see,
So you always stride at your true height
When smilingly reaching out a hand to me.

The Dancers in a Wicklow Field

I've stopped trying to guess what fate holds in store,
So let us for a moment leave our lives poised like this

On a makeshift dancefloor outdoors in a Wicklow field
As the last vestige of summer daylight starts to fade.

On our journey here we often got hopelessly lost,
With an intermittent phone signal, while our host

Genially issued directions, waiting at his remote gate
Until we found him, like we have found each other.

Here are friends we know and new friends to make,
But our host lures us from his party into this field

Where he has laid down boards of the sturdiest timber,
Rigging up lights and speakers for later in the night

When he hopes to cajole other guests to dance here.
But for now it's only us, happy to be his trail-blazers,

Laughing with him as he laughs and savours our joy
At dancing inelegantly in a darkening field amid hills,

Just miles from where my shy parents once kissed,
Eight decades ago, beneath trees in a hotel orchard,

So it feels that life has come full circle, after the complex
Twists endured before we could be here for one another,

Exultant in this moment, gladly making fools of ourselves
As we share with our dear friend this wondrous miracle

Of him watching us waltz with no need for lanterns or music,
Making our own magic by the light of the first evening star.

Acknowledgements

Acknowledgement is made to the editors of the following publications and radio programmes where many of these poems first appeared: *The Dark Horse, Long Poem Magazine, Bad Lilies, 14 Magazine* and *The High Window* in the UK; *Poetry Ireland Review, The Irish Times, The Sunday Business Post, Vox Galvia, The Honest Ulsterman, Sunday Miscellany* (RTE Radio 1), *The Poetry File* (Lyric FM), *Southword* and the anthology, *Local Wonders* (Dedalus Press) in Ireland; *The New Hibernia Review, Reading Ireland* and *'Dwelling During the Pandemic'* (Ohio State University) in the USA; *The Dalhousie Review* in Canada and the journal *InVerbis* in Italy.

'The Corporation Housing Architect' was printed as an introduction to a new edition of Ruth McManus's classic work, *Dublin, 1910 – 1940: Shaping the City & Suburbs*, published by Four Courts Press, and was first read by the author in a special podcast produced by MOLI (The Museum of Literature, Ireland) about the legacy of Herbert Simms.

'Eden Terrace' was made into a short film by the young Dublin filmmaker, Daniel Sedgwick, which premiered on the RTE Culture website. 'Men as Old as the Century' was commissioned as part of a project entitled *A Burning Tide* which The Irish Writers Centre curated and produced in association with Fingal County Council. 'Joseph Mary Plunkett's Rosary Beads' and 'After Grace' were among works written when the author was Writer in Residence at the National Museum of Ireland. The author expresses his thanks to Lorraine Comer, Head of Education at the National Museum of Ireland, Collins Barracks, and all of her staff. 'Written in a Church in Arezzo' was written while the author was a Fellow at the Civitella Ranieri Foundation. Sincere thanks to Dana Prescott and Diego Mencaroni, who made me welcome in the foundation's fifteenth-century castle in Umbria.

The author was grateful to be the recipient of the Anthony Cronin Award in Ireland and The Lawrence O'Shaughnessy Award for Poetry from the University of St. Thomas, Minnesota, in the USA. Both awards helped create the space in which these poems were written. Finally, the author would like to express his thanks to everyone at New Island Books involved in the publication of this collection and most especially to Stephen Reid for his judicious eye and shrewd wisdom.